EXCAVATING THE PAST

# THE INDUS VALLEY

Ilona Aronovsky and Sujata Gopinath

**H** **www.heinemann.co.uk/library**
Visit our website to find out more information about **Heinemann Library** books.

To order:
☎ Phone 44 (0) 1865 888066
▤ Send a fax to 44 (0) 1865 314091
▯ Visit the Heinemann Bookshop at www.heinemann.co.uk/library to browse our catalogue and order online.

First published in Great Britain by Heinemann Library, Halley Court,
Jordan Hill, Oxford OX2 8EJ,
part of Harcourt Education.

Heinemann is a registered trademark of Harcourt Education Ltd.

© Harcourt Education Ltd 2004
First published in paperback in 2005
The moral right of the proprietor has been asserted.

Editorial: Nicole Irving, Louise Galpine and Jeremy Smith
Design: Elaine Wilkinson
Picture Research: Ilona Aronovsky
Production: Edward Moore

Originated by Ambassador Litho Ltd
Printed in China by WKT

ISBN 0 431 14242 4 (hardback)
08 07 06 05 04
10 9 8 7 6 5 4 3 2 1

ISBN 0 431 14249 1 (paperback)
09 08 07 06 05
10 9 8 7 6 5 4 3 2 1

**British Library Cataloguing in Publication Data**
Ilona Aronovsky and Sujata Gopinath
Indus Valley. – (Excavating the Past)
934
A full catalogue record for this book is available from the British Library.

**Acknowledgements**
The publishers would like to thank the following for permission to reproduce photographs: Aachen University/Mohenjo-daro Research Project pp. **6** top, **8** ..., **11** top; Archaeological Survey of ...henjo-daro Research Project pp. **6** bottom, **15** centre and bottom, **40** centre; Art Archive p. **33** ...dgeman Art Library pp. **16** top and centre, **17** ...ft, **26** centre, **31** top, **34** bottom, **36** top, **37** ... British Museum pp. **27** bottom, **32** bottom, **33** ... Corbis p. **7**; Georg Helmes pp. **4** bottom, **9** ... bottom, **12** bottom, **24** bottom left, **30** top, ..., **43** top; JM Kenoyer/HARP pp. **9** top, **10** centre, **13** top, **14** top (artist reconstruction by Chris Sloan), **16** all, **17**, **18** all, **19** all, **21** top and centre, **23** all, **24** right, **25** all, **26**, **27** top, **28** centre and bottom, **29**, **30** bottom, **33** bottom, **34**, **35** all, **36** all, **37** all, **38**, **39** top, **42** top, **43** bottom; Luisa Ricciarini pp. **22** left and bottom right.

Cover photograph of Mohenjo-daro reproduced with permission of Corbis. The small photograph of the Priest King reproduced with permission of Harappa.

The publishers would like to thank J. M Kenoyer at Harappa Excavations Archaeological Research Project for his assistance with the preparation of this book.

Every effort has been made to contact copyright holders of any material reproduced in this book. Any omissions will be rectified in subsequent printings if notice is given to the publishers.

# CONTENTS

Any words appearing in the text in bold, **like this**, are explained in the Glossary.

# THE LOST CITIES OF THE INDUS CIVILIZATION

Near the town of Larkana, in Sindh, Pakistan, lie the remains of an ancient city once home to about 80,000 people. The streets and houses, now in ruins, were built between 4000 and 4500 years ago. It was not until the 1920s that archaeologists realized that it was the largest of several great cities, all part of a forgotten civilization that once existed in the area of modern-day Pakistan and northern India. Today, we know of about 2000 settlements in the Indus Valley belonging to an ancient civilization larger than ancient Egypt. They cover a territory the size of France – around 680,000 square kilometres.

▽ *The ruins of the High Mound at Mohenjo-daro city, built around 2500 BC.*

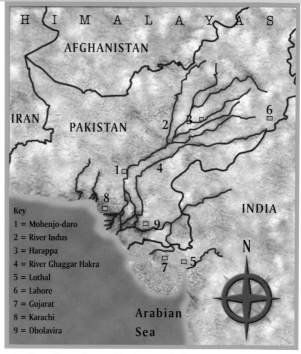

Key
1 = Mohenjo-daro
2 = River Indus
3 = Harappa
4 = River Ghaggar Hakra
5 = Lothal
6 = Lahore
7 = Gujarat
8 = Karachi
9 = Dholavira

△ *The Indus Valley civilization reached its greatest extent between 2600 and 1900 BC. This map shows its important cities.*

## Two great cities

The first city discovered by archaeologists is known as Harappa, named after the modern town which still lies on part of the ancient mound. Harappa is located next to the River Ravi, a **tributary** of the River Indus. About 590 kilometres downstream is the other large city, Mohenjo-daro. Some people say that the name means 'Mound of the Dead'. The terms 'Harappan culture' and 'Indus civilization' have been used because of these first two discoveries.

## EYEWITNESS

'East of Harappa was a ruinous brick castle. Behind us was a large circular mound, and to the west was an irregular rocky height, crowned with the remains of buildings... The walls and towers of the castle are remarkably high ...'

Charles Masson, from Narrative of Various Journeys in Balochistan, Afghanistan and The Panjab, written in 1842

## Two cities from one time

In 1872, Alexander Cunningham, the first Director General of the **Archaeological Survey in India (ASI)**, visited the ruins at Harappa to look for **Buddhist** remains. He was given a stone **seal** carved with writing never seen before. More seals with the unknown writing were found at Harappa, and the next director of the ASI, John Marshall, set up an excavation there to investigate. The dig began in 1920, led by archaeologist Rai Bahadur Daya Ram Sahni. At about the same time, in the ruined city of Mohenjo-daro, excavators found two more tiny stone seals, with the same type of writing as those from Harappa. Did this mean that both Harappa and Mohenjo-daro dated from the same period?

▽ *Seals like the one below were found in the city of Harappa and given to Alexander Cunningham, Director of the ASI, in 1872. They featured animals and had scripts on them, in a style that no one had seen before.*

## Matching the evidence

In 1924, Marshall, Sahni and another archaeologist called Rakhal Das Banerji met to compare finds from the two sites. They had found the same types of seals, bricks and red pottery with black designs. Marshall asked for help in understanding the seals. Experts on **Mesopotamia** told him that seals with the same writing had been found in ancient Mesopotamian cities, but it clearly was not Mesopotamian writing. Now they knew these seals must have come from the Indus Valley.

## Excavating the Indus Valley

From 1925–31, the largest excavations ever carried out in South Asia took place. In the first year, a team of archaeologists and 1200 workers began to uncover the walls and roofless buildings of Mohenjo-daro. Thousands of **artefacts** were found, including bronze tools, jewellery and engraved seals. At Mohenjo-daro the dig revealed large buildings on the highest mound, separate from an area of mounds named Lower Town. There have been excavations since, but around 90 per cent of the city remains unexcavated.

△ *The high mound at Mohenjo-daro, photographed from the air.*

### Harappa

Harappa was mainly excavated by M. S. Vats in 1926–34. The city had been badly damaged by brick-robbing in the 19th century, but Vats found thousands of artefacts, including **seals**, pottery and bronze tools. In 1986, a joint American-Pakistani project known as **HARP** began excavations that are still continuing today. Archaeologists have discovered how Harappa grew from a small farming village into a wealthy city.

◁ *Excavations at Mohenjo-daro. This photograph, taken in 1927, shows the discovery of a statue named the Priest King, in Lower Town.*

## WHO WAS M. S. Vats?

*Madho Sarup Vats was superintendent of the northern area of the Archaeological Survey of India. After excavating at Mohenjo-daro he worked at Harappa, leading the excavations there from 1926–34. He discovered two cemeteries and many important buildings, and then published the findings of the excavations in a series of large, illustrated books.*

## The beginning of the story

Several thousand years before the Indus cities dominated this area of South Asia, people had learned to farm the fertile plains of river valleys. Some small villages expanded into important trading towns, making luxury or valuable goods in metal, stone and shell. Then, around 2600 BC, many new cities were founded or rebuilt, in the style we call 'Harappan'. We call the people who lived in these cities the Harappans.

△ *The River Indus flowing through the Himalayas in northern Pakistan. The white deposits are silt which the river carries down from the mountains.*

## Pieces of a jigsaw

After the first excavations, archaeologists explored the valleys of the River Indus and found many more sites. Each year more sites are discovered, and there are now about 2000, but many more have been swept away by the River Indus.

In this book you will find out about the most important archaeological discoveries in the Indus Valley. You will discover how sites and objects have helped experts to understand the little-known civilization, and also how the latest archaeological techniques are being used to unravel the past.

### Archaeology Challenge

Bricks, pottery and artefacts of metal, shell, gemstones and minerals are virtually all that survive of the Indus civilization. Buried organic material, like wood or cotton cloth, usually rots away. This means that archaeologists must work out what buildings may have looked like and how people lived only from what does remain.

DID YOU KNOW? Every day 1 million tonnes of silt are carried by the River Indus.

**7**

# GREAT CITIES – MOHENJO-DARO

When archaeologists began excavating the site of Mohenjo-daro in the 1920s, they found an impressive brick city that was remarkably well preserved. House walls were still standing even though the roofs had long gone.

## Archaeology Challenge

In 1986, all of Mohenjo-daro was photographed from a hot-air balloon as part of a **UNESCO** project to look again at everything discovered there. Archaeologists can now compare these photographs with thousands taken in the 1920s and 30s.

Mohenjo-daro, which spreads over 250 **hectares**, is the largest Indus city found so far. It is ideally situated by the River Indus, so its people could travel along the river and trade with other cities and settlements along its banks. When the river flooded each spring it watered their crops, which meant food could always be grown for the city. But it was dangerous to live so near a river that could destroy everything when it flooded. It seems the city builders solved this by mounting all the buildings on top of artificial platforms. The earliest levels of the city may date to the Early Harappan period around 3500 BC. The upper part of the city dates from 2600–1700 BC.

## The High Mound

Mohenjo-daro is split into two parts – the High Mound (or **Citadel**), and the Lower Town. The High Mound is 18 metres high. It was originally surrounded by a massive mud brick wall and brick gateways. As people built houses on top of earlier buildings, the interior of the city grew higher, until the ground level reached the top of the city walls making it look like a huge platform.

▷ *An aerial view of the High Mound, Mohenjo-daro.*

▷ *The Great Bath at Mohenjo-daro is 12 metres long and 7 metres wide. Some archaeologists think religious ceremonies took place in the pool.*

One building on the mound, called the Great Bath, is made from layers of tightly fitting bricks. Bitumen (tar) between the outer layers made it watertight and so suitable for bathing. Archaeologists do not know how it was filled, but in the building they have found a well. The water emptied into a massive drain which ran below the bath.

Next to the Great Bath is another huge structure. In 1950, Sir Mortimer Wheeler re-excavated this and thought it was a **granary**. It has 27 brick platforms each the size of small rooms. Below them is a platform and **alcove**, which Wheeler thought was a loading bay for grain. But no trace of grain has been found here. Archaeologists today think it was either a great hall or a warehouse.

△ *The 'granary' at Mohenjo-daro.*

### The Lower Town

Most of the people of Mohenjo-daro lived in the Lower Town, 150 metres from the High Mound. Lower Town was built on several artificial mounds, which were rebuilt many times. In the rebuilding, houses were not destroyed. Instead, their walls were filled with mud bricks, to make foundations from which new walls could be extended upwards.

## WHO WAS Sir Mortimer Wheeler?

*Sir Mortimer Wheeler (1890–1976) went to India in 1944 as Director General of Archaeology. He introduced structured, scientific excavations and accurate recording by trained archaeologists. Wheeler visited Harappa, where he believed the High Mound was a Citadel. At Mohenjo-daro, he excavated the brick gateway of the Citadel mound. His most lasting influence on Indian archaeology was his now disproved theory for the decline of the Indus civilization. This was based on 39 skeletons found in Mohenjo-daro. Wheeler said they were victims of an **Indo-Aryan** invasion.*

## Unravelling a city

The Indus cities Mohenjo-daro and Harappa were built of **fired clay brick**. Some upper walls were made from mud (unbaked) bricks which stay cooler in hot weather. The bricks slotted neatly together, forming a strong **bond**. The bond is so strong that many excavated walls still stand today. The length of a brick was always double the width.

### The widest street in town

First Street is around 11 metres wide – large enough for two-way cart traffic. It probably ran north to south, right through Lower Town. The remains of craftwork and manufacturing industries are spread through the area.

▽ *First Street in Mohenjo-daro. A large drain of fired bricks, covered with* **oblong** *paving stones, runs beneath the street.*

## WHO WAS Sir John Marshall?

*Sir John Marshall was the first to recognize the importance of Rakhal Das Banerji and Daya Ram Sahni's work at Mohenjo-daro and Harappa. He was Director General of the ASI and excavated at Mohenjo-daro. He firmly believed the Indus Valley civilization was comparable with the ancient civilizations of Egypt and Mesopotamia. In the 1920s he wrote many newspaper articles ensuring that news of the exciting discoveries in the Indus Valley reached a wide audience.*

▽ *An aerial view of the remains of a house in Mohenjo-daro.*

## Visiting an ordinary house

Archaeologists have found that many houses had a similar design. The front door opened into a room like a hallway that went through to an open courtyard, where cooking and craft-working took place. The rooms were arranged around the courtyard, and light and air came from the doorways. Most houses had a bathing area made with watertight bricks, so that water flowed away through the street drains. Most houses also had a toilet, made from an old jar set in the floor. Waste was cleaned out and dumped in larger pits. Clean water came from deep brick wells, usually inside the houses.

## Life on the roofs

House walls were over a metre thick and because some stairways have survived, we know that they supported a second storey. The roofs were flat, with wooden beams and straw plaster. They may have been used as a place to chat with neighbours or as somewhere cool to sleep on a hot night.

△ *A well in a house in Lower Town.*

# GREAT CITIES – HARAPPA AND DHOLAVIRA

Harappa, in the Panjab province of Pakistan (590 kilometres from Mohenjo-daro), is the second largest city in the Indus Valley. The city spread over an area of 150 **hectares** and had a population of between 40,000 and 60,000. It was built on three separate mounds, each surrounded by massive walls.

## Excavating Harappa

The first excavators of Harappa were unable to discover the layout of the ancient houses because of brick-robbing. Bricks from earlier times had been re-used to build new houses. As a result, large parts of the city were destroyed and **artefacts** from different levels became mixed up. This means that a lot of valuable evidence has been lost forever. However, two cemeteries were found here, which were important as no cemetery has been found at Mohenjo-daro.

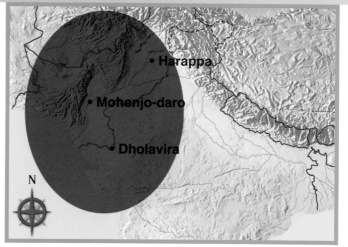

△ *Map showing location of Mohenjo-daro, Harappa and Dholavira. The red area shows the concentration of the Indus Valley settlements.*

▽ *Circular platforms in Harappa being re-excavated in 1998.*

◁ *A reconstruction of the city of Dholavira, which archaeologists discovered in 1967.*

People working for **HARP**, the joint Pakistan-USA research project, have been excavating at Harappa since 1986. Using modern techniques like **radio-carbon-dating**, they have been able to show how the mounds were built on through the centuries, and how Harappa grew from a small village into a wealthy trading and manufacturing city.

## Dholavira

Dholavira was founded between 2650–2550 BC. It spread over 100 hectares, and was built on Khadir Island in the Rann of Kutch in India, a dry wasteland that receives only 40 centimetres of rainfall a year. The whole city was built within square walls. Inside are fields which could be watered with rainwater that was stored in **reservoirs** inside and outside the city.

Dholavira is divided into three walled areas. The highest of the three has been described as a castle and a bailey. The castle is enclosed by massive stone and mud-brick walls and had gateways and towers. The bailey is a simpler building enclosed by fortified walls.

## Dholavira's Middle Town and Lower Town

Dholavira's Middle Town was also fortified. It contained spacious houses and open ground, which was probably used for markets or religious ceremonies. There were two or three large gates in Middle Town that allowed close communication with the Lower Town.

The Lower Town had densely packed, but well laid out houses with a main street running through the centre. Archaeologists have found evidence of craft workshops for shell-working, stone bead-making, pottery and copper-working that were located in some of the houses. Middle Town and Lower Town were surrounded with an outer fortification.

DID YOU KNOW? The bricks used to build any Indus city always have a ratio of 1:2:4.

## Inside Harappa

Harappa was well situated for trading. It was located near several land and river routes, which connected the northern highlands with the southern plains. This meant Harappa could control the transport of vital raw materials, like metal, wood and gemstones from far away, and send them to workshops in other cities in the Indus Valley.

## The city structure

This picture shows a reconstruction of a gateway in Harappa. The entrance to the city was through huge gateways, 3–4 metres high. The tops of the gateways may have had rooms that were probably used as lookout posts. Seals and weights have been found in the area, so the gateways may also have been checkpoints for goods coming in and out of the city. Beyond one gateway was a huge open area which may have been a market. Shell, **faience** and copper workshops have been discovered, as well as pottery **kilns**.

## Granary or storehouse?

A famous building in Harappa was first identified as a great 'granary' (shown right) by M. S. Vats. Nearby, seventeen circular brick platforms were discovered. Sir Mortimer Wheeler identified them as places where **grain** from the granary could be ground in the open air. New excavations by **HARP** excavators showed the platforms were inside separate rooms, belonging to different periods, and probably nothing to do with the granary. HARP has re-excavated the main granary building, and found nothing which could prove what it was used for.

## Dholavira's reservoirs

When the Indus people settled on Khadir Island, the city builders made sure they were prepared for the climate. Dholavira was designed to collect precious fresh water during the **monsoon season**. It was built on a slope between two storm-water channels designed to collect water from the annual downpour. The water flowed through a series of dams and channels into huge **reservoirs** carved out of solid rock. Archaeologists have also found a 4.25 metre-wide well, the largest yet discovered in the Indus Valley.

△ *One of the reservoirs at Dholavira, built deep into the rock below ground.*

### Archaeology Challenge

The Indus people built more than seventeen artificial reservoirs around Dholavira to collect rain water. Many of these lakes were huge, up to 590 by 170 metres. Besides builders, masons and brick-makers, it is likely that many ordinary people joined the construction teams. The city water supply was carefully designed so people could live in an area which was not suitable for farming. There must have been another reason for building a city there. Perhaps it was a good place near the coast for trading, manufacturing and getting raw materials?

### Public inscription

The **ASI** excavations led by R. S. Bisht made an exciting discovery in 1994. In a side room of the north gateway of the citadel was the only giant sized example of Indus writing every found. It is an inscription of ten symbols, each measuring 37 centimetres high. They were made of white **gypsum** paste inlaid in a wooden board, long rotted away, which must have fallen on its face. It may have been the name of the city or a title, that was mounted over the gateway.

# THE MYSTERY OF THE INDUS SCRIPT

To understand peoples of the past, archaeologists can usually turn to written evidence. Experts studying the Harappan culture have found 4000 objects with inscriptions, mostly discovered in the main cities of the Indus Valley. This script has been found on **seals**, pottery, metal tablets, tools and weapons. But specialists have not managed to **decipher** the Indus script, partly because all the inscriptions are very short. Another problem in decoding the script is we are still unsure what language it was written in. Yet the script and the **artefacts** that it is found on still provide clues about how life was organized in the Indus Valley.

◁ ▽ *Most of the Indus inscriptions appear on small seals. Wild animals such as tigers and rhinoceros are also common features of the seals.*

## WHO ARE Asko Parpola and Iravatham Mahadevan?

*Professor Asko Parpola of the University of Helsinki in Finland, and Dr Iravatham Mahadevan from India, are recognized as leading experts on the Indus script, one of the world's earliest writing systems. They both began working on the undeciphered writing 30 years ago, studying all the inscriptions and using in-depth knowledge of the languages, religions and cultures of South Asia and the ancient world. This has been very important in helping us to understand and interpret Indus discoveries.*

▽ Seal showing a unicorn found at Mohenjo-daro, dating from about 2200 BC.

## The seals and their writing

Over 3700 square and rectangular seals have been found in excavations. Most of these seals are made from soapstone and **faience**, and carved with human and animal figures. Real animals such as the humped bull, water buffalo, rhinoceros and elephant, are pictured on the seals. There is also an animal with one horn, which may be a mythical beast like a '**unicorn**'. It appears on about 60 per cent of all seals. Were these animals chosen as the emblems of groups of people living in the Indus Valley? Archaeologists are still trying to answer this question.

## Analysing the writing

More than 400 different signs appear in the Indus script. However, most inscriptions are short messages, containing five signs. We know the script was written right to left because many signs are cramped to the left edge of the seal where the writer ran out of space. If there are two lines of writing the second line goes back from left to right.

## Archaeology Challenge

In 1969, a team of Finnish scholars, led by Asko Parpola, used a computer to analyse all the Indus inscriptions. They discovered that each sign represented a whole word, or **syllable** of a word. Parpola then designed a table to show all the basic signs and how often they were used. This showed a pattern in the sign order. Parpola and another expert, Dr Mahadevan, thought this pattern was like the order in which people say words in a sentence. They think the Indus language was like Tamil, a modern language that is spoken by the people of southern India and Sri Lanka.

## Uses of the script

Archaeologists have found inscribed objects in different parts of the Indus cities, from empty houses to rubbish pits, to city gateways. Although the seals are found throughout a city, it does not mean that everyone knew and used writing. Only some sections of society would have had this knowledge. These would include rulers, religious leaders, city officials and traders.

△ *This square* **seal** *shows a male god with three faces sitting on a throne. He is wearing lots of bangles on both arms and an elaborate headdress. Symbols from the Indus script can be seen either side of the headdress.*

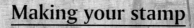

## Making your stamp

Indus **seals** may have been used to stamp the owner's identity or brand on a bundle of goods ready to be sold or exported. At Lothal, in India, 77 clay tags with impressions of seals have been found. This suggests that tags were attached to the bales of goods, probably before their export to **Mesopotamia**. We think this because many Indus seals and sealings have been found during digs in the ancient cities of Mesopotamia.

## The secret of the seals

There are several theories about how the seals were used. Merchants probably used seals to record their names and any official title that they might have. On the back of the seals was a raised, **perforated** knob which probably held a thick cord that could be hung around the neck or tied to the waist. These knobs were not very strong and often snapped. Archaeologists have found many damaged seals on the streets of Indus cities.

Seals were probably used for administrative purposes such as sealing parcels of goods. Experts also think stoneware bangles were placed in sealed containers for protection before they went into furnaces for **firing**.

### Indus astronomy?

One sign which appears a lot on the seals looks like a fish. In Tamil, the word *meen* or *min* means three things – fish, glitter and star. Language expert Asko Parpola thought the sign could refer to a star. When it is combined with other signs or numbers, it could mean the name of a star or a planet. Perhaps the people of the Indus were practising a form of astronomy?

### Numbers

According to language experts, numbers in the Indus script are shown as short strokes. The maximum number of strokes found on a seal is nine, which is arranged over two rows. Often sets of semi-circles are found with the strokes. These semi-circles are likely to represent tens in the Indus script.

Archaeologists studying the Indus Valley civilization have had to manage without evidence such as tomb paintings and written records, which can tell us so much about real people and the details of their daily lives. Yet we can still learn a lot from the way Indus cities were built, and the **artefacts** that people made.

## Archaeology Challenge

Seventy wells, 20 metres deep, have been found in Mohenjo-daro. Researchers worked out the average distance between them is 15 metres, so they have calculated the city had an amazing 700 wells! The well shafts made with wedge-shaped bricks were an Indus invention. The bricks locked together in a strong cylindrical shape which stopped them from caving in and kept the water pure.

## City builders

Vast numbers of people would have been needed to build cities the size of Harappa, Mohenjo-daro and Dholavira. There must have been many skilled workmen, including brick-makers, bricklayers, builders and carpenters in the Indus cities.

## City planners and engineers

Archaeologists believe that entire neighbourhoods of Mohenjo-daro were planned well before they were built. This is because the brick drains in Mohenjo-daro were designed and built so that they all linked together to allow waste water to flow out of the city. There would also have been architects and engineers who understood how to sink deep wells that collected clean water and which did not collapse.

▷ *Well shafts have been left standing like towers by the first excavators, who removed the layers of the buildings.*

## Traders, artists and craft workers

Many traders lived in the cities. Some of them may have lived in large houses in Lower Town, Mohenjo-daro, where many **seals** have been found. The goods they traded were made by skilled craft workers who also carved seals, and made shell ornaments and jewellery, metal objects, stone blades and tiny drills. Vast amounts of pottery were also produced for cooking, eating, drinking and storage. Some of it was beautifully decorated for special ceremonies.

## Rich and poor

In Mohenjo-daro it is sometimes hard to tell which houses belonged to rich people and which to poorer people. Some are large enough to be palaces, but they may have been homes for **extended families**. All houses, large or small, had clean water, a bathroom and the use of a toilet, joined to the city drainage system.

▽ Two examples of plans for smaller houses found in Mohenjo-daro.

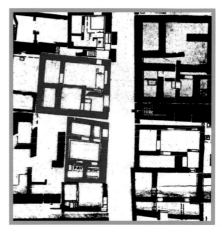

▽ An artist's impression of a large house in Mohenjo-daro, drawn by the excavator. It would have been owned by a wealthy family.

### Fantasy or Fact?

Many **figurines** have been found in rubbish pits, as if they were used and then thrown away. Female figures appear to portray a great range of different people, young and old. Perhaps they are models of what people hoped and prayed for, such as a successful future with lots of jewellery for a young bride?

## Clues to the past

Hundreds of small figurines of people, animals, birds and masks provide clues about people's daily lives and religious beliefs. They are usually hand-modelled in **terracotta**.

### Men and women

Archaeologists have found many male and female **figurines** in the Indus Valley which give clues about fashion and pastimes. Some adult male figures have small beards, while one of a small boy appears to hold a disc, like those excavated at Harappa. These are similar to ones used in a throw-and-chase game still played by children in Pakistan and northern India.

### Female models

Female figurines have been found in all shapes and sizes – some are slim, some fat and some nurse babies. Many female figures are wearing bangles and have different headdresses, such as cloth turbans. Some female figurines are adorned with flowers and lots of jewellery such as bracelets and decorated belts.

◁ *A figurine in terracotta, with an elaborate fan-shaped headdress.*

▽ *This bronze statue of a girl, found in a small house, is only 11 centimetres tall. She is wearing lots of bangles, and her hair is arranged in a thick plait.*

## Fun and games

Archaeologists have discovered many toys made for Indus Valley children. There are terracotta rattles, as well as a selection of wheeled animals. Bird figurines were made as whistles which may have been used in processions and festivals, and by children going hunting for birds with clay sling stones. Figurines on sticks may have been used in plays and entertainments.

▷ *Small horned masks may have been worn as **amulets**.*

### Dice and games

Cubical dice may have been a Harappan invention, usually made of sandstone or terracotta. Carved ivory tokens have also been found. These carved objects might be pieces used in games or in gambling, or fortune telling.

△ *Terracotta bird whistles were probably used to amuse children and may represent partridges or doves.*

## Jewellery for the rich

Fine jewellery was worn by wealthy people. **Carnelian** jewellery, thought to have come from the agate mines in Gujarat, was specially prized. Carnelian was chipped, polished, ground and baked twice to deepen the red colour. Very hard drills made from a special type of rock were used to drill holes through these incredibly long beads. Three hoards of jewellery in pots have been found, one from Allahdino (northeast of Karachi), and two from Mohenjo-daro. They included magnificent belts of long carnelian beads. Other jewellery included toe rings in silver, gold head bands, hollow gold bangles and anklets.

◁ *A necklace made from beads.*

## Faience

**Faience** is an artificial paste which can be given any colour, moulded and fired to make jewellery and ornaments. Faience from the Indus Valley was very hard and was used to make jewellery, tiny sculpted animals and tablets with the Indus script.

**HARP** project workers experimented with firing replica tablets of moulded faience. Using a special thermometer, they discovered the fire had to be around 940°C to make the faience so strong. The Indus faience makers worked without thermometers.

△ *J.M. Kenoyer, Director of HARP, places copies of faience tablets in a clay container for firing.*

## Archaeology Challenge

Pyrotechnology means controlling the exact temperature of fire to change a substance. If the temperature is too high or low, the artefact being fired will be spoilt. At Harappa, archaeologists have experimented to see how special **kilns** built to fire **terracotta** bangles worked. They stacked bangles inside sealed clay containers which were then put in a kiln. This kept the temperature stable and very high – producing super-hard terracotta, called stoneware. These stoneware bangles were engraved with the Indus script and they may have been worn by important officials.

▽ *Magnified photograph of tiny soapstone microbeads. These beads, which are only 1 millimetre in diameter, come from an elaborate hair ornament.*

## Jewellery for ordinary people

Rich people must have worn expensive jewellery, while other members of Indus society wore cheaper copies. Artificial stone beads made of faience that copied patterns on real gems have been found, as well as long beads made of terracotta, shaped like the carnelian ones worn by the wealthy.

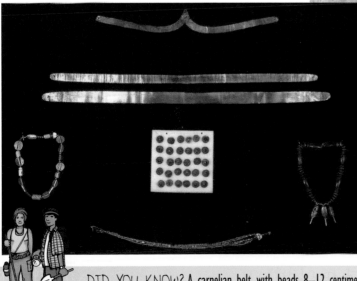

◁ *Most of this jewellery comes from two hoards discovered at Mohenjo-daro. The pieces are made of gold, silver and copper and colourful gemstones. Apart from necklaces and chains, there are also a selection of buttons that would have been worn by the wealthy.*

# FOOD AND DIET

**P**eople in Indus cities ate a wide variety of foods like cereals, meat, fish, vegetables and fruit. Archaeologists know this from animal bones and **carbonized grains** and seeds they have found in the cities. There are more clues from Indus art – pictures painted on pottery, carvings on **seals** and animal **figurines** showing the plants and animals that were part of the Indus world. There are even footprints left by cats, dogs and monkeys on clay bricks drying in the sun before firing, though such evidence does not prove these animals were eaten.

## Bones in the rubbish

Archaeologists have found animal bones near houses or in rubbish pits. These give valuable clues to the diet of the Indus people. At Harappa, archaeologists found that more than 50 per cent of all bones discovered were from cattle, 20 per cent of the bones from sheep and 5 per cent from goats. About a quarter of the animal bones at Harappa were from wild animals like gazelle and wild pig, so hunting must have been an important part of life. Some rhinoceros and elephant bones have also been found. Spears, arrows and clay slingshots would have been used to kill these animals for meat.

△ *The zebu (Indian humped bull), with its wide, curving horns may symbolize the leader of the herd. When carved on a seal, the zebu probably represents the top officials of Mohenjo-daro or Harappa.*

*▷ Terracotta models of rhinoceroses.*

## Clues from art

Archaeologists have discovered more about what people in the Indus Valley ate from the many different figurines they have found. There are models of animals like goats, sheep, rabbits and birds, as well as water buffalo, zebu, elephants, leopards and tigers. Many plants and animals appear as decoration on pots, seals and tablets, including date palms, fish, deer and peacocks.

### Archaeology Challenge

Excavations at Mehrgarh, on the highlands at the western edge of the Indus Valley, show how people's lives changed over thousands of years. Archaeologists have dated the first settlements to around 7000 BC from the animal bones and carbonized wood that they have found. From this evidence they think the people had learned to **domesticate** sheep, goats and cattle and to farm wheat and barley. Mehrgarh later became a large village, where people made pottery and jewellery. They also traded gemstones with other villages and towns across the Indus Valley region. Mehrgarh became a flourishing town.

## Grains and seeds

Grains that have been accidentally burnt do not rot, and can survive for thousands of years. Excavating house floors and rubbish pits in many Indus sites, has shown the most common grains eaten by the Indus people were wheat, barley and millet. They also grew lentils, chickpeas, mustard and sesame seeds.

*▷ Carbonized grains which have survived thousands of years have been found on house floors in Harappa.*

## Farming

▷ *Wheat was grown in the fertile fields of the Indus Valley.*

From the list of plants that were grown, archaeologists have worked out that Indus Valley farmers cultivated their fields twice a year. Some of these crops have to be planted in the autumn, and some in the summer. This meant that fresh food was always available.

## Ploughing the fields

A plough pulled by bulls was probably used to prepare the land. However, the only evidence of the use of a plough are small clay models, and a field excavated at Kalibangan, with the furrows still in the ground.

▷ *Copper and bronze plates were probably only used by wealthy Indus city families.*

## Cooking ware

There was a wide range of pottery, designed for cooking and storing food, as well as for drinking and eating. There were also copper plates and pots for the rich. The cooking pots had a wide, stable base to sit on the fire and spread the heat evenly. Most dishes were made from clay but bronze pots were used to boil and stew different foods. Large, rounded pots kept liquid cool.

## Archaeology Challenge

Archaeologists have long been interested in the number of fish skulls found together in a pit in a small coastal town called Balakot. There are hundreds of fish skulls but no bones. By talking to local fishermen, archaeologists can guess what happened. Today the fish are caught, and then are salted to preserve them. The people at Balakot must have cut off the heads and thrown them away, and then salted the fish and sent it hundreds of kilometres up the river to the cities.

## Fishing

The fish is one of the most common symbols in the Indus script. A picture painted on a tiny **sherd** found in Harappa may show how the people caught fish. A man is shown carrying two round fishing nets, standing near a larger net. These clues have given archaeologists the idea that fish may have been an important food, especially for people living in cities. The use of nets means that large quantities of fish were probably caught. Rivers and lakes near the cities had plenty of fish after the yearly floods.

## Spicing up life

Archaeologists think Indus Valley people ate many different fruits and vegetables including mustard greens, peas, melons and gourds. Other foods available in the region may have included honey, palm sugar, dates, jujube (like a plum), figs, gourds, okra, cucumber and capers, and grapes, nuts, apples and apricots brought from the western highlands. Plants like ginger, turmeric, cinnamon, coriander and garlic come from this part of South Asia, and may have been used to add spice to meals.

# TRAVEL AND TRADE

The Indus people were keen traders. They travelled long distances for materials such as copper and bronze for luxury goods. River boats brought metal ores, giant conches (shells), flint and gemstones to the city workshops. Villages on river banks and land routes to mountain regions grew to become important trading posts and manufacturing centres. Harappa and Mohenjo-daro were the largest of these.

## Travelling around

Rivers in the Indus region were used to transport goods thousands of kilometres. Clay models of flat-bottomed boats have been found at Harappa and Lothal. Travelling downstream, pushed by the current, a boat could travel many kilometres in just a few days. Archaeologists think loaded boats going up-river had sails and may also have been pulled along by men and animals walking on the banks. Sheep and goats with small saddlebags were used to bring tin, silver, gold and gemstones from the highlands around the Indus Valley.

△ *Traditional two-wheeled bullock carts and flat-bottomed ferry boats are used today to transport goods along the River Indus.*

## By sea to the lands of the west

Two **seals** from Mohenjo-daro show flat-bottomed boats that may have carried goods to the coast. Sailboats with **keels**, made from wood or tightly plaited reeds, would have taken goods across the sea. No boats survive but bits of tar, used to waterproof boats, with impressions of boat planks have been found on beaches on the sea route to **Mesopotamia**.

▷ *This seal found in Mohenjo-daro, shows a flat-bottomed boat. These boats had sails as well as long oars.*

▷ *The metal ores, copper and tin were brought long distances to make these copper and bronze tools and weapons.*

## Control of trade

Archaeologists have found seals which provide us with important clues about Indus trade. Many seals have inscriptions on them that may be names. Archaeologists think this could mean that seals were used to label trade goods so that people knew to whom they belonged, or to show they had given the city rulers their correct taxes.

◁ *Cubical weights found in Harappa. The smallest weight could accurately weigh things as light as 0.87 grams.*

### The importance of weights

Archaeologists have found no evidence that the Indus people used money. Instead, it is likely that people **bartered** for everyday goods they wanted. Weights were used to judge and compare the value of trade goods or bulk items like grain. Some archaeologists think that weights were also used to work out tribute – amounts of grain villages had to send to the city rulers. At Harappa, many weights have been found in rooms at the city gateway, where trade goods coming in and out of the city were probably controlled.

### Fantasy or Fact?

*Lothal is thought to have been an important port of the Indus Valley. A large tank at the site was first thought to be a dock but was actually a reservoir for fresh water. Small boats could have docked on the river bank, as they still do today, and large boats would stay out in the bay. From here boats could have sailed west along the coast, and on towards the Gulf of Khambhat.*

## Trade with Mesopotamia

Archaeologists know that people in the Indus Valley traded with other countries because they have found Indus-style **artefacts** across the region. These include clay tablets found in **Mesopotamia** with the name Meluhha written on them in **cuneiform writing**. Archaeologists think that Meluhha was the Mesopotamian name for the Indus Valley. The tablets record trade goods, including **carnelian**, monkeys, a peacock, wood and a dog. One tablet boasts of ships arriving from the Indus region.

### EYEWITNESS

"The ships from Meluhha, the ships from Magan, the ships from Dilmun he made tie up alongside the quay of Agade."

*King Sargon (2334–2279 BC), boasting of the range of ships anchored in the docks at his capital, Agade, in Mesopotamia*

## Bullock carts

Two-wheeled wooden bullock carts were used by local people, but no traces of full size carts have been found. Instead many model terracotta carts have been discovered. At Harappa, Sir Mortimer Wheeler found wheel ruts, 1.6 metres apart, proving that the carts used there were large vehicles designed to carry heavy loads over uneven surfaces. Some carts carried people, while others took heavy loads, which could be rolled on and off.

## Trade with Oman

Harappan artefacts have also been found in Iraq, Bahrain and Oman, where there are ancient copper mines. Pottery **sherds**, some with Indus script scratched on, litter the beaches of Oman. These come from very large storage jars with narrow bases. The jars could be neatly stacked in a ship's hold. Archaeologists have recently tested the pottery and the results have shown that the clay came from the Mohenjo-daro region.

## Importing goods

Mesopotamian artefacts have not been found in Indus cities. However, Mesopotamian tablets do refer to the export of wool, incense and gold to Meluhha. Some finds in the Indus Valley also suggest trade with parts of Central Asia. Bronze pins with animal-shaped heads and other popular images, such as eagles, have also been found in Harappa.

▷ *Storage jars similar to this one were used to transport goods like grain and oil.*

### Guest houses

Cities may have provided guesthouses for travelling merchants. Some archaeologists believe that a building found in Lower Town, Mohenjo-daro, that has two rows of rooms equipped with bathrooms, may have been a type of motel for merchants. Finds discovered here may have been left by the visitors, the artefacts include copper weighing pans, seals and a tiny **faience** squirrel, shown above.

### Archaeology Challenge

Some archaeologists suggest that human **figurines** with different headgear and hairstyles show that people from Harappa and Mohenjo-daro belong to many different classes and **ethnic** groups.

# RULERS AND RELIGION

For 700 years the Indus civilization dominated a huge area of South Asia. Despite this, however, we do not know the name of one person, or one ruler who lived in the Indus region, nor do we know about events that may have happened there. The **seals**, writing and weights show the cities were part of a trading network, but who controlled it? Did powerful kings rule the cities? If the Indus script could be **deciphered**, would we find the answers? We can only follow the clues we have, until more evidence is discovered.

## Planned cities – built by rulers?

Archaeologists know that the city of Mohenjo-daro was carefully planned and maintained over a long period of time. They know this from the careful and complex way the streets were laid out, and how drains were built to keep the whole city clean.

## Rulers' meeting place

Did city rulers live or work in the highest mound? The high mound at Mohenjo-daro had massive walls around it and so did the mounds at Harappa. Most archaeologists think they were built to control who came in and out. High walls would also impress people with the power of the rulers, as well as protecting a city from river floods. The high mound at Mohenjo-daro contained unique buildings. It had a very large paved hall which may have been a meeting place for the rulers of the city.

*◁ Burial of an adult man in Harappa. The man was found wearing a long necklace of 340 soapstone beads.*

## Religious ceremonies

Archaeologists do not know if any building in Mohenjo-daro was a temple. However, they are fairly certain that religious ceremonies led by rulers and traders and grand processions must have taken place there. It is also believed that the gateways to the mounds at Harappa were designed for this purpose.

## Cemetery sites

Archaeologists have discovered only a few hundred Indus graves. Most people were buried in coffins, but some bodies may have been disposed of in other ways. One cemetery which dates from the time of the Indus civilization has been excavated at Harappa. There are other small cemeteries at Kalibangan and Dholavira but so far the cemetery at Mohenjo-daro has not been found.

## Buried jewellery

Women and some men were buried with their bangles, and some had beads and necklaces. Bangles may have been worn for religious reasons. In one grave a man was found wearing a hair ornament at the back of his head made of many strands of tiny micro-beads.

### Archaeology Challenge

There is nothing in the Indus Valley like the treasure-filled graves of the pharaohs and nobles of ancient Egypt. Perhaps the Indus people held different beliefs about the afterlife and so were not buried with many personal grave goods.

### Grave goods

The people buried in the excavated cemetery in Harappa were probably well off. However, they only took household pottery with them. Archaeologists think the pots may have held food and water as offerings for their journey into the next life.

△ *The scene on this seal may represent a sacrifice.*

## Ritual and worship

One Indus **seal** (left) shows a **deity** with a horned headdress and bangles on both arms, standing in a **pipal** tree looking down on a kneeling worshipper. The pipal is a sacred tree in India, and its leaves also decorate pottery. A human head rests on a small stool. The deity is surrounded by a giant ram and seven figures in procession. These types of seals represent important events or stories that we can never understand without reading the script.

## Who was the Priest King?

The small statue, found in 1927 in Lower Town, Mohenjo-daro, was given the name of Priest King by archaeologists. The trefoils on the cloak, once filled with red, are known to be religious symbols in **Mesopotamia**. This symbol appears on other Indus artefacts, including a fragment of a bull. The Finnish language expert, Asko Parpola, suggests the trefoils symbolize stars or hearth fires of Gods in the sky, and they may have been worn on the cloak of a royal person. It would be natural for rulers and important people in ancient times to wear religious symbols. However, if he was a royal person it cannot be proven.

▷ *The statue known as the Priest King is only 18 centimetres tall. It is the most famous of several stone statues of males found at Mohenjo-daro.*

## The waters of life

The Great Bath at Mohenjo-daro was probably a place for special religious ceremonies. The pool was surrounded by a **verandah** with pillars. There was also space for processions to move around the pool. Some archaeologists suggest that it may have been where ceremonies for important leaders or rulers took place. Perhaps rulers entered the pool seeking **purification** by sacred water? Alternatively, the waters may have symbolized the new life brought by the annual floods.

## Priestly duties

Iravathan Mahadevan believes that a sign which looks like a jar or pot with handles, represents a container for holy liquid. When it is combined with a stickperson carrying a yoke it means an important official who is bearing the burden of office and who also has priestly duties. Other stickpeople are combined with a sign that looks like a spear, which may indicate a warrior leader.

## The mythical unicorn

Many seals found in the Indus region show a **unicorn**-like animal. One archaeologist has suggested this is a legendary beast which protected the people of a mighty clan of traders in this world and and the next. The unicorn is always shown standing next to an object which may be an offering stand or sacred **brazier** for incense.

# THE DECLINE OF THE INDUS CIVILIZATION

The Indus civilization flourished for around 700 years. Around 2000 BC, Harappan cities began to decline. Between 1900 and 1700 BC many towns and villages were deserted. Parts of Mohenjo-daro were no longer lived in and gradually the whole city was abandoned. People continued to live in Harappa and many refugees from the dried up rivers to the east came to Harappa to live. Groups of people living along the now dry Ghaggar-Hakra River, abandoned their settlements and moved to Harappa or new lands in the east.

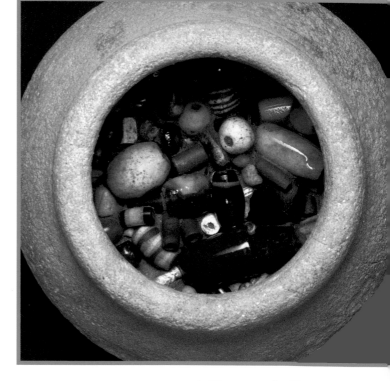

## Deserted cities

Archaeologists do not know if the cities were deserted gradually or as the result of a sudden disaster. However, they have found evidence that life in many cities was changing for the worse.

## Signs of decline

At Mohenjo-daro, buildings on the High Mound were divided into small workshops and the Great Bath was built over. At Dholavira, ordinary people moved into what had been important public buildings and at Harappa the mounds became overcrowded. Drains in cities were not cleaned and became blocked. Streets were abandoned and clogged with rubbish, including the bodies of dead animals. In Mohenjo-daro the skeletons of 39 people were found in streets and buildings.

△ The person who filled this bead pot in Harappa, around 1700 BC, had collected stone beads from earlier times, as well as faience and the first known glass bead in South Asia.

## Hidden treasures

Three hoards of precious jewellery were hidden under house floors, at Mohenjo-daro and Allahdino, at this time. These included **carnelian** belts, and gold **fillets**. They may have belonged to a jewellery merchant or wealthy family, but we do not know what happened to the owners.

◁ *Different faience beads (shown actual size) found buried at Harappa.*

## Trade and crafts decline

Trade between all the areas of the Indus civilization broke down. The supplies of copper and lapis lazuli as well as sea shells could no longer be delivered. Luxury crafts, such as making long carnelian beads and shell-carving, were no longer practised. At Harappa, workshops made **faience** beads instead, and the first ever glass beads. Local trade grew while trade beyond the Indus region stopped.

## Abandoned trade

At Lothal the building that may have been a warehouse was abandoned and later burned down. In **Mesopotamia** evidence of trade with the Indus Valley disappeared. There were no **seals**, no luxury Indus **artefacts** and no mention of Meluhha in the tablets. Stamp seals and cube weights were no longer made or used. The use of the script was discontinued, and the writing and the seals used by the most powerful people forgotten.

### Archaeology Challenge

Recent archaeology has shown that some people abandoned their lives in the Indus cities and went to farm in new lands along the Ganga and Yumuna rivers. They began to grow summer crops like rice and millet, instead of only winter crops like wheat and barley. They used local materials and their knowledge of pyrotechnology to produce glass. The first glass beads in South Asia, were made in Harappa.

# Why the Indus civilization declined

We will probably never know why this flourishing civilization came to an end. However, archaeologists have suggested different reasons to explain the decline.

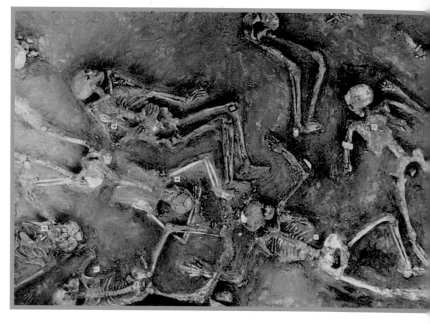

▽ *Some of the skeletons found by Harold Hargreaves, one of the first excavators at Mohenjo-daro.*

## Aryan invasion

A famous, early explanation was based on the 39 skeletons found in Mohenjo-daro. The archaeologist Sir Mortimer Wheeler believed the people had met a violent death in a massacre caused by people known as **Indo-Aryans**. Wheeler thought they had invaded Mohenjo-daro, killed the inhabitants and then had gone on to conquer the land. But archaeologists today reject this explanation. If there had been an invasion in the Indus Valley, there would also have been signs of burning and destruction to Mohenjo-daro and all the other great cities.

## The changing course of rivers

Some archaeologists think that rivers helped bring about the decline of the Indus Valley civilization. When the ancient Saraswati (or Ghaggar-Hakra) river ran dry, the villages along its banks that depended on it for trade and for their agriculture were abandoned. The capital was similarly affected. Some archaeologists think that earthquakes blocked the River Indus causing Mohenjo-daro to flood, while others think the Indus changed course, leaving the city high and dry. We cannot prove whether either theory is correct, but some archaeologists say changes in the environment are not enough to explain the decline in the Indus civilization.

## The end of trade with Mesopotamia

Around 1800 BC, there were major changes in **Mesopotamia**. Cities to the north became more powerful and traded with cities in Central Asia, not with the Indus Valley. This may have caused a crisis for powerful Indus traders. But we do not know how important trade by sea was compared with trade through the Indus lands.

△ *Sailing boats on the Indus River. Around 1800 BC, overseas trade between the Indus civilization and western Asia stopped. Due to its own political and economic problems, Mesopotamia was unable to trade with the Indus region. As a result, the Indus economy may have suffered a major setback.*

### Archaeology Challenge

It is 50 years since Sir Mortimer Wheeler suggested the skeletons of Mohenjo-daro met a violent death. They have all since been re-examined by Kenneth Kennedy, a forensic archaeologist. He discovered that only two skeletons had wounds. The wound on one was old and the other was already healing, because bone had grown back, proving it had happened some time before. There is nothing to prove how these people died.

## The fall of the rulers?

Another theory to explain the end of the Indus civilization is the breakdown of administration and the end of the ruling classes. Evidence like the skeletons left unburied, damaged statues such as that of the Priest King at Mohenjo-daro, and hidden hoards of jewellery may indicate the city was going through bad times. The statues may have been smashed to show disrespect for rulers. Perhaps the rulers were no longer in charge? The problem is that the bodies and damaged statues could easily be found in any partly uninhabited city, especially where there was no one in control.

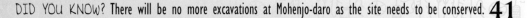

# INDUS ARCHAEOLOGY TODAY

We have learned a great deal about the Indus civilization since Charles Masson first noticed the Harappa mounds in 1826. Although the early excavations provided us with valuable information about how the towns were planned, the architecture and arts and crafts, we knew little about the daily life of the people. However, since the 1970s, archaeologists have used modern techniques to research the environment, agriculture and occupations of the people.

## Field surveys

Field surveys are when archaeologists walk the countryside to discover ancient sites. A mound of earth with **artefacts** on the surface, like pottery **sherds** or bricks, shows a probable site. In the 1990s, M. R. Mughal identified 201 sites of the Indus civilization in the districts of Sindh and Cholistan in Pakistan, many near the dried up River Ghaggar-Hakra.

## Hot-air balloon photography

In the 1980s, **UNESCO** sponsored new research at Mohenjo-daro and it was declared a **World Heritage Site**. Michael Jansen produced an accurate map of the whole site with the help of balloon photography. The site was marked out with a grid and photographs taken in each square with a camera hanging from the balloon. The new photographs were then compared with a huge collection of pictures taken by the first excavators. These have all been mapped and transferred to computers for analysis.

△ *An archaeologist fixes a camera to a hot air balloon. Aerial photos helped archaeologists to discover ancient flint mines in the Rohri Hills.*

△ *Expert flint workers sliced off these blades on the left leaving the pieces on the right, called cores.*

In the 1990s, a team of archaeologists from Pakistan and Italy used field surveys and balloon photography to investigate the Rohri Hills in Pakistan. This revealed many flint mines and workshops for making stone blades. Using chemical analysis, they proved that most of the flint blades in all Indus cities came from here.

## Archaeology Challenge

As we do not have any written records from the Indus Valley which could tell us about the history of the cities and important events, finding out the dates when Indus cities were built and what changes took place through the centuries is very important. Archaeologists today can use modern methods of stratigraphy and **radio-carbon-dating**. Radio carbon dates have helped archaeologists pinpoint the time when most of the important Indus cities were built (or rebuilt) to a period of 100–150 years before 2600 BC. This tells us there were great changes going on in the region. In a similar way archaeologists can tell when people stopped living in the cities.

## Climate and vegetation

The climate and environment of the Indus valley have been studied using scientific techniques such as analysing pollen grains found in layers of **silt** from lakes. Under the microscope scientists can see if the plants that grew in ancient times are different from those that grow now. This also tells them if the climate has changed since ancient times.

▽ *This plate found in a cemetery at Harappa dates from 1900 BC. It has a design of blackbuck antelope, combined with an older design of the trefoil or three circles.*

## The legacy of the Indus civilization

A thousand years after the Indus civilization, people had developed the lands of the Ganges and Yamuna rivers to the east, and much of Southern India for farming and city life. This happened because knowledge of agriculture, metalwork, creating jewellery and providing clean water and sewage disposal continued after the decline of the Indus civilization.

# TIMELINE OF THE INDUS VALLEY CIVILIZATION

The history of the Indus Valley is usually divided into three periods by archaeologists: Early Harappan, Harappan and Late Harappan. The first signs of an Indus Valley civilization appeared around 5000 BC, based on village farming. Then, around 2600 BC, the Indus civilization experienced an explosion in its population growth, with the formation of cities including Harappa and Mohenjo-daro. The final period of history, around 1900 BC, marked the start of a decline in the Indus Valley civilization.

**More than 2 million years BC**
Early hominids living in the northern Indus Valley, flake stone tools and discard them.

**500–100,000 years BC**
Lower Palaeolithic Stone Age people discover flint at Rohri Hills. This area continues to be used for flint mining in later periods.

**30,000–10,000 BC**
Upper Palaeolithic Stone Age people settle in the Indus Valley. They live in caves and use stone tools to hunt for food. They also gather fruit and nuts.

**About 6,500 BC**
The first villages are established in the Indus region. The Neolithic (New Stone Age) people grow wheat and barley and also keep cattle, sheep and goats. They continue to hunt animals and gather fruit and nuts. The first villages develop and comprise oblong, mudbrick houses with several rooms, some of which are used as storage areas.

**5000–1300 BC**
The Indus Valley civilization develops. Archaeologists have divided the civilization into three sub-divisions – the Early Harappan, Harappan and Late Harappan Periods. These sub-divisions refer to the different phases of development of the Indus Valley civilization, from early village to a fully developed city, and finally to the period of its decline.

### 5000–2600 BC
### Early Harappan Period

Some villages develop into towns which are planned on a grid pattern, with roads running northwest to southeast. Many towns are enclosed by mudbrick walls. Some important towns in this period are Kalibangan, Banawali and Kot Diji.

### 2600–1900 BC
### Harappan Period

Important cities such as Harappa, Mohenjo-daro and Dholavira develop. These large cities have many public buildings, markets and even some craft workshops.

Important crafts develop, such as bead-making, seal-making and producing decorated pottery and metal tools. Cities become important trade centres, bringing raw materials to craft workshops and shipping finished products to different parts of the Indus Valley and **Mesopotamia**.

The Indus script is invented. Different types of houses start to be constructed. Houses range from one room dwellings to large, grand double-storey buildings with wells, courtyards and bathrooms.

Some archaeologists believe that in this period the Indus civilization is ruled by different competing elites, who may have been merchants, landowners or priests. However, we have no conclusive proof to support this theory.

### 1900–1300 BC
### Late Harappan Period

The Indus Valley civilization gradually declines. There is a breakdown in the organization of the cities, with no one in control.

Trade with Mesopotamia ends. Use of the script disappears by the end of the period. The Indus civilization breaks into several regional cultures that gradually spread out over Gujarat and the fertile plains of the Ganga-Yamuna river valleys to the East.

# TIMELINE OF INDUS ARCHAEOLOGY

### 1826

James Lewis, a British Army deserter, travels through the Panjab district of Pakistan, posing as an American engineer, under the false name Charles Masson.

On his travels, he discovers the ruins of a vast city, with the remains of a brick castle. The city was later identified as Harappa. He records the presence of this site in his book, *A Narrative of Various Journeys in Balochistan, Afghanistan and the Panjab*.

### 1831

Sir Alexander Burnes, a young British explorer, begins to map the Panjab region. On his visit to Harappa, Burnes recognizes the archaeological importance of the site.

### 1850

Railway engineers start to destroy the site at Harappa. Vast numbers of bricks are removed from the ancient mounds to construct railway beds.

### 1853

Sir Alexander Cunningham visits Harappa for the first time. Cunningham, Director General of the **Archaeological Survey of India (ASI)**, visits Harappa as part of his survey of ancient **Buddhist** sites visited by Chinese pilgrims.

### 1872–73

Sir Alexander Cunningham begins excavations at Harappa. The excavations fail to reveal any Buddhist remains. However, he discovers ancient pottery and stone tools from an earlier period. Cunningham also finds the first Indus **seal**. It shows a **unicorn**-like animal and an inscription in an unknown script. This seal arouses the interest of scholars all over the world.

### 1911

Devadutta Ramakrishna Bhandarkar discovers the site at Mohenjo-daro.

### 1920–26

Sir John Marshall, Director General of the Archaeological Survey of India undertakes extensive excavation at Harappa and Mohenjo-daro. Excavations reveal a building they called the Granary (at Harappa and Mohenjo-daro) and the Great Bath at Mohenjo-daro. In addition a bronze figure of what might have been a dancing girl was found.

### 1924

On 20 September 1924, the *Illustrated London News* announces the discovery of an early Indian civilization.

### 1927–31

Sir Ernest Mackay, a trained Egyptologist, is appointed as a Special Officer to the Archaeological Survey of India. During his excavations at Mohenjo-daro, Mackay discovers the plans of the Great Pillared Hall as well as the plans of houses. He also recovers a soapstone seal depicting the figure of a **deity** sitting in a special pose.

### 1946

Sir Mortimer Wheeler, becomes Director General of the Archaeological Survey of India, and undertakes the excavation of the city walls and fortifications at Mohenjo-daro. Wheeler developed his famous **Indo-Aryan** massacre theory, based on 39 skeletons excavated around the city which had never received a proper burial.

### 1967

J. P. Joshi, Director General of the Archaeological Survey of India, discovers the important site of Dholavira. Dholavira is the largest Indus site in India.

### 1969

Asko Parpola, a language expert from Finland, attempts to **decipher** the Indus script.

### 1977

Indian linguist I. Mahadevan, attempts to decipher the Indus script.

### 1986–90

George Dales, Director and J. Mark Kenoyer, Field Director of University of California, Berkeley, Archaeology Project, conduct excavations at Harappa. For the first time, scientific survey methods and analytical techniques are applied to materials from Harappa.

### 1990–94

R. S. Bisht conducts his excavation at Dholavira. His work reveals the plan of the city, and the presence of seventeen **reservoirs** and a stadium. The most important discovery is an inscription, which is thought to be the sign of the city.

# GLOSSARY

**alcove**
A square or rounded hollow area in a room wall which can have a shelf.

**amulet**
A small piece of jewellery, often worn as a charm to protect against evil.

**Archaeological Survey of India (ASI)**
Organization founded by Alexander Cunningham, in 1861. Its aims were to make a record of all the historic buildings and ancient ruins in India.

**artefact**
Any object made or used by humans.

**astronomy**
Knowledge of how the stars and planets move which people in ancient times used for directions or to work out the time and dates.

**barter**
Trade without money by swapping goods people agree are worth the same.

**bitumen**
A thick, sticky, oily tar found in the ground, which dries hard and is waterproof.

**bond**
The way bricks are arranged to fit together so that walls do not fall over.

**brazier**
A container for burning wood.

**bronze**
A hard metal made by mixing copper with tin or arsenic.

**Buddhism**
The religion founded by Siddartha Gautama, the Buddha, about 500 BC.

**carbonized**
When something has been burnt so dry that it does not rot.

**carnelian**
An agate (gemstone) which when heated becomes a deep red colour and can be made into a shiny jewel.

**citadel**
A city defended by high walls to prevent enemies from attacking.

**cuneiform writing**
Wedge-shaped 'letters' used in ancient writings and inscriptions.

**decipher**
To work out the meaning of something.

**deity**
A god or goddess.

**domesticate**
Keeping animals for meat, milk, skin or muscle power.

**ethnic**
Belonging to a group with a particular culture, language or race.

**extended family**
A large group of family members who all live together or very near to each other.

**faience**
Type of ceramic paste that can be coloured, made into different objects and then baked hard.

**fertility, fertile**
Able to have lots of babies, or rich land where plants grow well.

**figurines**
Clay models

**fillet**
A headband.

**fired bricks**
Mud bricks baked hard in hot fire.

**grain**
The dried seeds of plants we eat like wheat and barley.

**granary**
A place for storing threshed grain.

**gypsum**
A soft white mineral used to make cement, paint, glass and fertilizer.

**HARP**
Abbreviation for Harappa Excavations Archaeological Research Project.

**hectare**
A metric unit equal to 10,000 square metres.

**Indo-Aryan**
People who spoke an ancient language related to modern Hindi, Urdu or Punjabi.

**keel**
The bottom of a ship.

**kiln**
Special oven used to bake pottery, tiles and bricks.

**manufacturing**
Making things that people use or need.

**Mesopotamia**
An old name for modern Iraq and the ancient civilization which flourished there, 3200–500 BC.

**monsoon season**
Summer months in South Asia when great torrents of rain fall.

**mortar**
A thick paste that dries and is used to stick bricks together.

**mud bricks**
Bricks made of clay in a mould, left to set hard in the sun, but not fired.

**oblong**
Four-sided shape with two sides longer and two sides shorter.

**perforated**
Small holes made in an object.

**pipal**
A fig tree sacred in India.

**pollen record**
Pollen from plants survives thousands of years. Archaeologists can tell which plant it came from under a microscope.

**purification**
Making yourself clean, by washing.

**radio-carbon-dating**
A way of working out how long ago an animal or plant died. After something dies tiny amounts of a substance called, carbon-14 slowly gets less and less. Because scientists know how long this takes, they can work out how long ago an animal or plant died.

**raw materials**
Things like rocks, earth, and wood that are used to make artefacts.

**reservoir**
Large natural or manmade lake used as a water supply.

**seal**
A carved object used to stamp an impression into clay. The impression is then attached to an object to show who owns it or who sent it.

**sherd**
A piece of broken pottery.

**silt**
Earth or mud carried by water.

**South Asia**
The part of Asia in which India, Pakistan, Bangladesh, Nepal and Sri Lanka are situated.

**stoneware**
Clay fired at such high temperatures that it becomes incredibly hard.

**syllable**
Part of a word containing only one vowel.

**technique**
A special skill people use.

**terracotta**
A clay which turns reddish-brown when fired.

**trench**
A long deep pit. An archaeological trench is like a downward slice through layers of ground with the lowest being the oldest.

**tributaries**
Smaller rivers that flow into a large river like the River Indus.

**UNESCO**
Abbreviation for the United Nations Educational, Scientific and Cultural Organization.

**unicorn**
A mythical beast with one horn.

**verandah**
Part of a building that has a roof and pillars but no walls.

**World Heritage Site**
Site or structure that is internationally recognized as being important and deserving protection.

# FURTHER READING

**History Quick Reads: Indus Valley**, Helen Cannam (Anglia Young Books, 2003)

**History Opens Windows: The Indus Valley**, Jane Shuter (Heinemann Library, 2003)

**Make Your Own Ancient Artefact The Indus Civilisation Cart Kit**, modelling kit by Ilona Aronovsky (HEC, 1999)

**Settlements of the Indus River**, Rob Bowden (Heinemann Library, 2004)

**The Young Oxford Book of Archaeology**, Norah Moloney (Oxford University Press, 1995)

## WEBSITES

www.ancientindia.co.uk
Site that displays the small collection of Indus artefacts owned by the British Museum, with educational activities.

www.harappa.com
Extensive site with slide shows of artefacts, excavations and the latest discoveries, maintained by Indus Valley archaeologists.

www.moenjodaro.org/
Site created for an exhibition in Japan, with computer-generated reconstructions of Dholavira.